WHAT DO YOU CALL YOURSELF?

The Power of Scriptural Affirmation

I0176605

GRACE ADEOLA AYOOLA

SYNCTERFACE™

WHAT DO YOU CALL YOURSELF? THE POWER OF
SCRIPTURAL AFFIRMATION

ISBN: 978-0-9933860-9-1
Copyright © January 2019 by Grace Adeola Ayoola
All Rights Reserved

Published in the United Kingdom by

SYNCTERFACE™

**Syncterface Media
London**

www.syncterfacemedia.com
info@syncterfacemedia.com

Cover Design by Syncterface Media

Dedication

I dedicate this book to my friend Joan Dunn and to those who have been awakened to the eternal truth that whatever you call yourself is what you will become

Contents

Foreword

*I*n *"What do you call yourself? – the power of scriptural affirmation"*, Grace is asking each believer to re-examine daily the confessions they silently and audibly make about themselves because the statement, "what you call yourself determines your destiny" is very true.

Our heavenly Father Himself lends credibility to this truth by changing the names of Abram and Jacob. He renamed Abram as Abraham which means *"Father of many nations." (Genesis 17: 5)*. Similarly, Jacob's name was changed to Israel meaning *"One who struggled with God and man and prevailed." (Genesis 32:29)*. Both of them reaped bountiful benefits from their new names.

Grace also insightfully expands on many key points as she looks into the importance of the words "I am" in helping believers gain victory over the enemy. She stresses the reintroduction of the unlimited power of the Holy Spirit and the difference He makes in our quest for victory over the enemy. The Holy Spirit is the one that wroughts miracles with supernatural and inexplicable authority. The Holy Spirit is the one who anoints and transforms. With the help of the Holy Spirit we can add power to our confessions to make them fiery and fruitful.

The link between our confessions and worship also demonstrates the deep passion Grace has for the worship of the Father, a theme that goes right to the centre of Grace's ministry. Our most powerful confessions are those of Thanksgiving, Praise and Worship to the Father who is able to do more than we can think.

Grace has produced another excellent work.

Dr. Tokunbo Ayoola Archie. MD

PART I

Confessions create your future

Chapter 1

What you call yourself matters

Through faith we understand that the worlds were framed by the word of God, so that things which are seen were not made of things which do appear.

Hebrew 11:3

Words have power because words have energy and therefore, they will manifest assuredly. Positive words have the power to change things, to revitalize our relationships, finances, and our health. The words we speak are commands that shape our destiny. We are each therefore what we confess ourselves to be.

Jesus said in John 6:63b: "*...the words that I speak unto you, they are spirit and they are life*". He spoke and the dead came back to life. He spoke and opened the eyes of the blind. He spoke and the lame could walk.

The energy in God's word pervades all space and animates all things. The energy in God's word are forever alive, and active. The Bible in Hebrews 1:3 says that God *"upholds all things by the WORD of His power"*.

The Creator spoke the world into existence. He said: *"Let there be light and there was light"* Genesis 1:3. Every time he said: *"Let there be…"* creation followed. As children of the living God who called those things that be not as though they were, we are to speak life and energize the world around us.

Negative words have the power of destruction. This is clearly demonstrated in the book of Numbers, chapters 13 and 14, which gives account of the result of evil report that was brought back by some of the spies who were sent to view the Promised land. God told Moses, *"Say unto them, as truly as I live, saith the Lord, **as ye have spoken in mine ears, so will I do to you:** Your carcasses shall fall in this wilderness…"* Numbers 14: 28-29. Brothers and sisters, please note that those who brought back evil report perished in the wilderness. Only Caleb and Joshua who brought back good report of the land were able to go to the Promised land.

The principle of confessing with our mouths is a fundamental principle of the Christian faith. Confession is a necessary step for salvation as written: *"… with the heart man believeth unto righteousness and with the mouth, confession is made unto salvation"* Romans 10:10b

When anyone speaks negative words, every kind of lack, limitation and discord will manifest. Unfortunately, this is what many people are doing all the time. The law of sowing and reaping is no respecter of persons but as Charles F. Haanel wrote in his book titled The Master Key, "*This law as well as every other law is no respecter of persons, but is in constant operation and is relentlessly bringing to each individual exactly what he has created.*"

Sowing and Reaping the Word of God

There are many scriptures in the Bible that support the potency of sowing words to reap the manifestation of the same words. In the parable popularly known as the Parable of the Sower described in Mark 4, Jesus equated the sowing of the seed to the sowing of the Word. The principle He was trying to pass across was the principle of sowing the word of God through speaking it. The confessions we make every day are seeds planted in our lives to grow and bear fruits ready for harvest at the appointed time. Our spoken words become our reality in the future. What we sow in thoughts, words and deeds is what we will reap in our experiences. What we imagine in our hearts and constantly confess will determine our future. Why not start confessing the future you desire with your words.

The assurance we have in this process is rooted in the fact that God instituted a process of seed-time and harvest.

> [22]*While the earth remaineth, seed-time and harvest, cold and heat, summer and winter, day and night shall not cease.*
>
> *Genesis 8:22.*

God is committed to making what you sow bear fruit. He reinforced the message for the children of Israel by establishing a process that required the children of Israel, by law, to recognize a feast of harvest. Seeds need to be sown for a harvest. The sower then patiently waits for the season of the harvest.

> [14] *Three times thou shalt keep a feast unto me in the year.*
>
> [15] *Thou shalt keep the feast of unleavened bread: (thou shalt eat unleavened bread seven days, as I commanded thee, in the time appointed of the month Abib; for in it thou camest out from Egypt: and none shall appear before me empty:)*
>
> [16] *And the feast of harvest, the firstfruits of thy labours, which thou hast sown in the field: and the feast of ingathering, which is in the end of the year, when thou hast gathered in thy labours out of the field.*
>
> [17] *Three times in the year all thy males shall appear before the LORD God.*
>
> *Exodus 23:14-17.*

Every Word is a Seed

Many don't realise how powerful their words are and how much attention God pays to the words that proceed from our mouths. For example, in *Numbers 14*, after crossing the Red sea, the children of Israel encountered challenges that caused them to murmur against Moses the prophet and Aaron. When read carefully, the response from God was quite shocking. Even though the children of Israel were not talking directly to God or praying like many of us would when going through challenges, God still heard them. They were complaining to leadership about God and God heard them. God does not require our permission to listen to what we say. He knows our thoughts before we speak. Look at God's response.

> *26 And the LORD spake unto Moses and unto Aaron, saying,*
>
> *27 How long shall I bear with this evil congregation, which murmur against me? I have heard the murmurings of the children of Israel, which they murmur against me.*
>
> *28 Say unto them, As truly as I live, saith the LORD, as ye have spoken in mine ears, so will I do to you:*
>
> *29 Your carcases shall fall in this wilderness; and all that were numbered of you, according to your whole number, from twenty years old and upward which have murmured against me.*
>
> Numbers 14:26-29.

Every word that comes out of your mouth has an express route to God whether you are in an attitude of prayer or not. Their confessions and actions extended a journey that should have taken forty days to forty years. Many people ceaselessly talk about the problems they encounter in life, but this story is clear proof that murmuring and negative confessions delay favor, blessings and breakthroughs. Dwelling on the negative and repeatedly confessing problems inadvertently invite more problems. Our victory lies in positive confessions even during negative circumstances.

There are many references in the Bible that point to the grave dangers of inappropriate use of our tongue through negatively spoken words. Here are some:

> *36But I say unto you, that every idle word that men shall speak, they shall give account thereof in the day of*

judgement. [37] For by thy words thou shalt be justified, and by thy words thou shalt be condemned

Matthew 12: 36-37.

[2]If any man offends not in word, the same is a perfect man, and able also to bridle the whole body

James 3:2.

[23]Whoso keepeth his tongue keepeth his soul

Proverbs 21:23.

[6]The tongue is a fire, a world of iniquity: so is the tongue among our members, that it defileth the whole body, and setteth on fire the course of nature; and it is set on fire of hell

James 3:6.

[8]The tongue can no man tame, it is an unruly evil, full of deadly poison

James 3:8.

Wherefore, my beloved brethren, let every man be swift to hear, slow to speak, slow to wrath.

Ecclesiastes 5:2; James 1:19.

Conclusion

LOVE and the WORD are the most powerful forces in the world. The Father is LOVE and the son is the WORD. It is therefore not surprising that the words we speak have energy and are as volatile and powerful as atomic bombs.Words can heal or kill, help or hinder, create or negate, hurt or soothe, humiliate or elevate.

Leaders have used words to transform nations. Other

leaders have used words to start wars and change the course of history.

Rumi said;

"Raise your word not your voice. It is rain that grows flowers not thunder".

Joyce Meyer said;

"Words are containers for power, you choose what kind of power they carry".

Betty Eadie said;

"If we understand the power of our thoughts, we would guard them more closely. If we understand the awesome power of our words, we would prefer silence to almost anything negative. In our thoughts and words we create our own weaknesses and our own strengths".

Bishop Oyedepo said;

"A closed mouth is a closed destiny".

Brothers and sisters, you can change the course of your life with the kind of words that you speak. We need to choose our words carefully because our words shape our destiny. Your destiny is in your tongue so be careful how you use your tongue.

Most of the confessions in this book start with the active, creative and dynamic words "I am". This is to assist you to call yourself by your proper name. "I am" is the real Christ Mind in each person. So when you confess with that appellation, you are calling yourself by your true name and therefore attracting the best things in the Universe to yourself.

Chapter 2

Three Power Boosters for your Confessions

Thou shalt also decree a thing, and it shall be established unto thee:...

Job 22:28

*N*ow that we understand how important the words we speak are, I want to show you three ways you can very quickly increase the potency of your confessions through practices that you, most likely, already engage in but did not realize their impact in the context of confessions.

Expressing Confessions through Thanksgiving, Praise and Worship

I believe that thanksgiving, praise and worship are the most dynamic forms of confessions anyone can make. I say, "dynamic" because these are confessions that can be offered through a plethora of psalms, hymns, spiritual songs and even poems. If we look close enough, we will find that most people have one thing or another to thank God for. For example, the act of offering thanks from our lips by using the words, "Thank you Jesus" is such a powerful thing. We are recognizing God and making a conscious decision to be thankful and God hears that.

We know that God created us for His glory (*Isaiah 43:7c*) and that He inhabits the praises of His people. (*Psalm 22:3*) So, as soon as we switch the words that come out from our lips to those that praise and ascribe greatness to God, He shows up on the scene. Remember, if God will show up to the murmurings of the children of Israel, He will certainly show up when praise and worship is offered to Him.

When we are in His presence with thanksgiving, praise and worship, He fills every cell in our body with His light and vitality which enables us to be bold and courageous as we are lifted out of anxiety, fear, doubt and every false thinking. Our consciousness is elevated to the level of all possibilities and we begin to reign with Christ in heavenly places above all principalities and evil powers. It is my prayer that every believer would experience this indescribable type of anointing while confessing the praises and adoration of our Father and God.

The Power of 'I am' Confessions

The Bible, in *Romans 12: 2*, admonishes us to be transformed by the renewing of our mind. After accepting Christ and receiving the baptism of the

Holy Spirit, the next level of transformation is to be aware that as His children, we are co-creators on this earth. Our Creator is the GREAT I AM THAT I AM and we His children are the "I am" on the earth today. The "I am" is the silent, all-wise partner in each of us. It is the source of infinite strength, health, wealth and power within us. The Bible says, "Let the weak say I am strong...". Because of what the Lord has done for us at Calvary, we can now decree a thing and it will be established. (*Job 22:28*) This realization should awaken the sleeping giant inside us. You can change your life by what you affix to the "I am."

Jesus understood this concept of His identity with His "I am." Some of the confessions He made using the words "I am" is a testament to the depth of understanding He had regarding His identity.

Here are some of His confessions:

I am come in my Father's name (John 5: 43).

I am the light of the world (John 8:12).

Before Abraham was, I am (John 8:58).

I am the Way, the Truth and the Life (John 14:6).

I am the door of the sheep (John 10 :7).

I am the good Shepherd (John 10:11).

I am the living bread which came down from heaven (John 6.51).

I am the true vine and my Father is the husbandman (John 15:1)

There is power in the "I am" for those who have received Christ as their Savior. The living water flows into each soul that accepts Jesus as Lord. That living water is the Word Incarnate. As it is written "You have been born again not of seed which is perishable but imperishable, that is, through the living and enduring word of God" (*1 Peter 1:23*). Jesus is the Living Word that is imperishable.

Accept Jesus if you have not already done so, to receive the Living Water, the Way, the Truth and the Light from the Almighty Creator.

We were all created to give God pleasure by attaining to the full stature of Christ and by pushing back darkness on this earth. To this end, Apostle Paul prayed:

> *17 That the God of our Lord Jesus Christ, the Father of glory, may give unto you the spirit of wisdom and revelation in the knowledge of him:*
>
> *18 The eyes of your understanding being enlightened; that ye may know what is the hope of his calling, and what the riches of the glory of his inheritance in the saints,*
>
> *19 And what is the exceeding greatness of his power to us-ward who believe, according to the working of his mighty power,*
>
> *Ephesians 1:17-19.*

What a great prayer and how I wish that all believers would pray this prayer every day. We need to pray that the eyes of our understanding may be enlightened to know who we are in Christ. We need to define ourselves accurately to be empowered to function maximally and achieve greatness.

We are all fearfully and wonderfully made in the image of our Creator. When we identify as "I am" and begin our confessions with "I am", a fourth dimension is introduced with accompanying power and potency. Jesus lived in the power of His I am while on earth. He is our Master and we ought to follow his example. There is more power in our confessions when we add "I am."

Maintaining Your Confessions In The Face of Adversity

Our thoughts come out in the words we speak and these thoughts and words create our circumstances. Instead of repeatedly making negative statements, it is more powerful and beneficial to adopt a word-based, optimistic approach in any situation to redefine our perspective.

The story of the Shunamite woman in the Bible gives us a perfect example to reinforce this point. Her only son had just died, and she decided to look for Prophet Elisha who had previously prayed for the birth of the now dead child.

When Elisha saw her approaching, he said to Gehazi, "Run now I pray thee and say to unto her, Is it well with thee? Is it well with your husband? Is it well with the child?" She did not lament the death of her son to Gehazi, she answered, "It is well" (2 Kings 4:26). She had purposed not to let the deeply distressing situation affect the words she spoke.

Elisha went back with her and the woman's confession of, "It is well", ensured that the power of

God was activated and what she believed God for became her reality. Her dead son was raised from the dead. Her faith and confession preceded her miracle.

As children of God, we should always remember that every word is a catalyst that is either taking life from or giving life to the experiences of our life Remember, life and death are in the power of the tongue.

Brothers and sisters in Christ, do you know that adversity is an adversary?

Here is the consolation, the Word says

> *²² But if thou shalt indeed obey His voice, and do all I speak; then I will be an enemy unto thine enemies, and an adversary unto thine adversaries .*

> *Exodus 23:22.*

Here is how Jesus conquered the adversary who tried to introduce adversities into his mission on Earth. Jesus used the words "It is written..." to conquer the adversary. Let us learn to do the same.

Here are some examples:

It is written:

> *¹³He has delivered us from the power of darkness and translated us into the Kingdom of His dear Son.*

> *¹⁴In whom we have redemption through his blood, even the forgiveness of sins.*

> *Colossians 1: 13-14.*

It is written:

> [37] In all these things, we are more than conquerors through him that loved us.
>
> Romans 8:37.

It is written:

> [19] Behold, I give unto you power to tread on serpents and scorpions, and over all the power of the enemy and nothing shall by any means hurt you.
>
> Luke 10:19.

It is written:

> The accuser is cast down, who accused us before God day and night. And we overcame him by the blood of the Lamb and by the word of our testimony.
>
> Revelation 12: 10-11 (paraphrase)

Remember the assurance we have in Job 22:28 that says, "Ye shall decree a thing and it shall be established."It is best to use biblical confessions to defeat the adversary and the adversities he brings our way.

Chapter 3

The Place of Thanksgiving and Adoration

Even every one that is called by my name: for I have created him for my glory, I have formed him; yea, I have made him.

Isaiah 43:7

God created man as an expression of His workmanship and used Praise and Worship as a means for man to maintain his connection with his creator, God. A realization of this gives meaning to life and existence. It is the failure to serve and worship God that creates a barrier between man and his Creator.

In multiple instances in scriptures, God always desired that the children of Israel will serve him but they never saw things the way God did. They preferred to do their own thing and were repeatedly called "stubborn", "disobedient", and "ungrateful". The prophet Jeremiah even showed his desperation at the situation when He said:

> [11] *Hath a nation changed their gods, which are yet no gods? but my people have changed their glory for that which doth not profit.*
>
> [12] *Be astonished, O ye heavens, at this, and be horribly afraid, be ye very desolate, saith the LORD.*
>
> [13] *For my people have committed two evils; they have forsaken me the fountain of living waters, and hewed them out cisterns, broken cisterns, that can hold no water.*
>
> *Jeremiah 2:11-13.*

In the book of Acts, Stephen called the children of Israel "stiff-necked and uncircumcised in heart". No doubt then, and very much in this present time, there have been damning writings against the people who were disobedient to God. Nevertheless, God, in His infinite wisdom, always went the extra mile to reconcile His people back to himself. When His people were in captivity in Israel, he reached out to them by sending them prophets who were tasked with delivering the people of God.

Moses and Aaron were instructed to go and tell Pharaoh, that the LORD God of Israel, The I AM THAT I AM says *"Let my people go, that they may hold a feast unto me in the wilderness." (Exodus 5:1).*

It is clear from this scripture that the purpose for the deliverance of the children of Israel from bondage is so that they may go and worship God, the Great I AM in the wilderness, free from oppression after which they will be led to the land of promise. Similarly, the purpose of our salvation is so that we may be set free from Satan and become "a royal priesthood" to offer spiritual sacrifices to our God, the Great I AM (*1 Peter 2:9*).

The Bible says people perish for lack of knowledge. Indeed, many people are ignorant of the fact that it is only worship that brings us to the presence of God. Adoration of God allows us to have a rich spiritual experience that purifies what we are grateful for and energizes us.

We enter the gates of the Living God with thanksgiving, proceed into His Courts with praise and enter His presence with worship to be gifted and transformed. What a privilege to be able to go boldly to the throne of the Almighty I AM! Let us review the lives of some people in the Bible who were transformed because they were obedient to the command to worship their Creator.

God told Abraham to go and sacrifice his only son in the wilderness. Abraham obeyed and made the journey to the mountain with Isaac and two of his young men. *"And Abraham said unto his two young men: Abide you here with the ass; and I and the lad (Isaac) will go yonder and worship." (Genesis 22:5)*. Abraham knew that the purpose of the journey to the mountain was to worship God. As a result of Abraham's loving obedience, God provided a ram for the sacrifice in lieu of his son. His willingness to sacrifice his son to the Almighty I AM has immortalized his name as the favored one who has been blessed mightily.

Let us look at the example of David. How did David qualify to be the man after God's heart? Remember that although he was willing and ready to build a

Temple for the LORD, he was not allowed to build the Temple because he had shed a lot of blood. How did a "bloody man" become the man after God's heart? The answer is that David was a worshiper. The scripture says that David praised God seven times a day. (*Psalm 119:164*). When the Ark was being moved to the house of Obed Edom, David danced with all his might and offered burnt offerings and peace offerings unto God. (*1 Chronicles 15*). It is written also that on that day, David first delivered a psalm into the hand of Asaph and his brethren, to thank the LORD. (*1 Chronicles 16:7*).

When God sent a pestilence upon the children of Israel because of their sins David planned to sacrifice praises to God on behalf of the children of Israel. God sent a prophet to David to go to the threshing floor of Araunah and build an altar to offer his sacrifices to the LORD. Araunah offered to make the piece of land a gift to David but David refused and said: "*No, but I will surely buy it of thee at a price: neither will I offer burnt sacrifices unto the LORD my God of that which cost me nothing.*" (*2 Samuel 24:24*). His love for God made him refuse the gift; he said he could not give God that which costs him nothing. David deeply appreciated the mercy that God had shown him throughout his life as recorded in the Psalms he wrote. His name was entered in the Book of Records because he lived to worship God; he made the worship of God the central theme of his life. This gave David a place in the Book of Records, the only man referred to as a "man after God's heart" as a result of his loving obedience to praise and worship the Great I AM with his whole heart and with all his strength.

Finally, let us acknowledge another person whose name was immortalized because of her exemplary worship: the woman with an alabaster box of very precious ointment recorded in *John 12:3-8; Matthew 26:6-13*; and *Mark 14:3-10*. She is another example of perfect worship.

She gave an expensive gift to the Lord Jesus (recorded to be more than three hundred pence). She gave it willingly and joyfully. The fact that the disciples complained that it was a waste did not stop her from pouring the oil on the feet of Jesus. She gave the gift with humility (*wiping the Lord's feet with her hair*). Jesus said, "*... wherever this Gospel is preached throughout the world, what she has done will also be told, in memory of her!*" *(Matthew 26:6-13)*. This woman, like Abraham and David, entered the Book of Records by honoring the Messiah unreservedly.

God is looking for such worshippers for it is written: "For the eyes of the LORD run to and fro throughout the whole earth, to show Himself strong in the behalf of them whose heart is perfect towards him." (*2 Chronicles 16:9*). The LORD will strengthen the heart of those whose hearts are fully committed to Him. It is also written: "Eye has not seen, nor ear heard, nor have entered into the heart of man, the things which God has prepared for them that love him." (*1 Corinthians 2:9*).

This is an invitation to you to be in God's Hall of Fame by offering daily worship to the uncreated, self-sustaining, immortal God, the I AM THAT I AM.

**IF YOU WISH TO JOIN THE ARMY OF
WORSHIPPERS, MAKE THE SACRED COMMITMENT
ON PAGE 102**

Chapter 4

The Holy Spirt makes all the difference

*But ye shall receive power, after that the Holy Ghost is
come upon you:...*

Acts 1:8

Without the Holy Spirit, the Church of
Jesus Christ will have no power to
operate on the earth. The Holy Spirit is the person
that energizes words and makes them potent. Jesus
described the spiritual nature of the words that he
spoke. He said;

> *63 It is the spirit that quickeneth; the flesh profiteth
> nothing: the words that I speak unto you, they are spirit,
> and they are life*
>
> *John 6:63.*

Jesus' words were spirit and life because the
Holy Spirit had worked on them. Right from the
beginning of scriptures to the end, the Holy Spirit

has played important roles in being the agent of change and empowerment.

The Holy Spirit at Creation

The Holy Spirit was the one that brought order to the primordial chaos.

> [1] *In the beginning God created the heaven and the earth.*
>
> [2] *And the earth was without form, and void; and darkness was upon the face of the deep. And the Spirit of God moved upon the face of the waters.*
>
> [3] *And God said, Let there be light: and there was light.*
>
> *Genesis 1:1-3.*

Without the Holy Spirit at work, chaos and disharmony will exist but notice in *verse 3* that it was in this atmosphere of the Spirit that the words *"Let there be light"* were uttered. Confessions are most powerful when uttered with the inspiration of the Holy Spirit.

Scriptures were Inspired by the Holy Spirit

It is obvious from scriptures that the words of past and present-day prophets were and are only as powerful as the degree to which they were and remain inspired by the Holy Spirit. Words were not spoken lightly. Words were spoken with intent just like God did at creation.

> [16] *All scripture is given by inspiration of God, and is profitable for doctrine, for reproof, for correction, for*

instruction in righteousness:

2 Timothy 3:16.

[21] *For the prophecy came not in old time by the will of man: but holy men of God spake as they were moved by the Holy Ghost.*

2 Peter 1:21.

There are many examples of Prophets whose words testified of the impact the inspiration of the Holy Spirit had on the words they spoke. Look at what some of them had to say.

- Prophet Elijah talked about the still small voice (*1 Kings 19:11-13*)

- Prophet Micah said, in *Micah 3:8*, "But truly I am full of power by the spirit of the Lord, and of judgment, and of might, to declare unto Jacob his transgression, and to Israel his sin"

- Prophet Isaiah, speaking many years ahead of the birth of Jesus, spoke the powerful and prophetic words that are still echoing through eternity.

[6] *For unto us a child is born, unto us a son is given: and the government shall be upon his shoulder: and his name shall be called Wonderful, Counsellor, The mighty God, The everlasting Father, The Prince of Peace.*

[7] *Of the increase of his government and peace there shall be no end, upon the throne of David, and upon his kingdom, to order it, and to establish it with judgment and with justice from henceforth even for ever. The zeal of the LORD of hosts will perform this.*

Isaiah 9:6-7

Jesus and the Holy Spirit

Jesus, the great Shepherd and Bishop of our souls, did not start the work of the ministry until He was baptized with the Holy Spirit. At His baptism, the Holy Ghost descended in a bodily shape like a dove upon Him, and a voice came from heaven, which said, *"Thou art my beloved Son; in thee I am well pleased" (Matthew 3:17)*. He was led by the Holy Spirit to fast and pray for forty days. After that, Jesus was enabled to launch his ministry on earth *(Luke 4:1,14)*. Thereafter, Jesus chose his twelve disciples, ministered to people, and performed miracles by the power of the Holy Spirit.

As it is written,*"Jesus returned in the power of the Holy Spirit into Galilee...."* (Luke 4:14). In the Synagogue in Nazareth Jesus read what the Holy Spirit already prophesied about him in the book of Isaiah.

> [18] *The Spirit of the Lord is upon me, because he hath anointed me to preach the gospel to the poor; he hath sent me to heal the brokenhearted, to preach deliverance to the captives, and recovering of sight to the blind, to set at liberty them that are bruised,*
>
> [19] *To preach the acceptable year of the Lord.*
>
> *Luke 4: 18-19.*

This passage from the Bible confirmed beyond any doubt that Jesus was operating under the power of the Holy Spirit.

The Church and the Holy Spirit

Jesus spoke emphatically concerning the Holy Spirit before his crucifixion. Jesus said: *"Nevertheless I tell you the truth. It is expedient for you that I go away; for if I go not away, the Comforter will not come unto you; but if I depart, I will send Him unto you." (John 16:7)*.

After his resurrection, Jesus again gave his disciples a promise of the gift of the Holy Spirit saying: *"Ye shall receive power after the Holy Ghost is come upon you; and ye shall be witnesses unto me both in Jerusalem, and in all Judea and Samaria, and unto the uttermost part of the earth" (Acts 1:8)*. He laid emphasis on the power of the Holy Spirit when He said:

> [12] *I have yet many things to say unto you, but ye cannot bear them now.*
>
> [13] *Howbeit when he, the Spirit of truth, is come, he will guide you into all truth: for he shall not speak of himself; but whatsoever he shall hear, that shall he speak: and he will shew you things to come.*
>
> [14] *He shall glorify me: for he shall receive of mine, and shall shew it unto you.*
>
> *John 16:12-14.*

Jesus warned his disciples concerning the unforgivable sin which is a sin to the Holy Spirit:

> [31] *Wherefore I say unto you, All manner of sin and blasphemy shall be forgiven unto men: but the blasphemy against the Holy Ghost shall not be forgiven unto men.*
>
> *Matthew 12:31.*

Jesus requested the Father to send the omni-present

Holy Spirit whose influence could be felt across all corners of the earth. As Jesus had promised, the Apostles received the power of the Holy Spirit after the resurrection of Jesus. The Holy Spirit descended on the disciples to inspire, empower, anoint, and lead them. The change was dramatic. For example, immediately after the outpouring, Peter gave a sermon then converted 3,000 souls into the fold of Christ. In *Acts 3:1-8,* Peter and John, at the gate of the temple, raised a lame man. Before this outpouring of the Holy Spirit, there was no evidence at all of any powerful signs of leadership in Peter. This was the same Peter that denied Jesus during the night of his trials.

The Jews must have been absolutely convinced that the death of Jesus would be the end of their problem. Imagine the horror of the ruling Council of the Jews when they got word that the Apostles had been empowered to preach, convert, and perform miracles after the baptism of the Holy Ghost. It is recorded in the scriptures that the Word of God increased; the number of disciples multiplied in Jerusalem greatly, and a great company of the priests were obedient to the faith! *(Matthew 6:7).* These were all due to the influence of the Holy Spirit.

Chapter 5

The Inner man:
The Root of Potent Confessions

...Christ in you, the hope of glory:

Colossians 1:27

*C*onfessions of Praise and Thanksgiving to God (*The Father, Son and Holy Spirit*) is something that needs to come from our hearts. It should not just be a mental or emotional response but a spiritual response from deep inside our being. It should be a heart-felt response from a spiritual person to God our Creator. Isaiah the Prophet spoke about this and, interestingly, Jesus also quoted him.

13 Wherefore the Lord said, Forasmuch as this people draw near me with their mouth, and with their lips do honour me, but have removed their heart far from me, and their fear toward me is taught by the precept of men:

Isaiah 29:13.

7 Ye hypocrites, well did Esaias prophesy of you, saying,

> [8] This people draweth nigh unto me with their mouth, and honoureth me with their lips; but their heart is far from me.
>
> [9] But in vain they do worship me, teaching for doctrines the commandments of men.

Matthew 15:7-9.

A lot of people struggle with this concept of letting Praise and Thanksgiving come from the heart because some do not even know that the real person is firstly, spiritual after which they possess a soul and live in a body. I was amazed to discover a report in the Telegraph, one of the newspapers in the United Kingdom, titled *"Bright Flash of Light Marks Incredible Moment Life Begins When Sperm Meets Egg ."*[1] Here is an extract from the article:

"Human life begins in bright flash of light as a sperm meets an egg, scientists have shown for the first time, after capturing the astonishing 'fireworks' on film.

An explosion of tiny sparks erupts from the egg at the exact moment of conception...Not only is it an incredible spectacle, highlighting the very moment that a new life begins, the size of the flash can be used to determine the quality of the fertilised egg."

When we consider what the bible says in, *John 1:9*, we see that the scriptures almost exactly describe what the scientists have discovered. Jesus is described as the true light that *"lighted every man."* This means without Jesus, the spirit of man cannot enter the egg in the womb of the mother. It is also

---

1 https://www.telegraph.co.uk/science/2016/04/26/bright-flash-of-light-marks-incredible-moment-life-begins-when-s/

written, "*The spirit of God hath made me and the breath of the Almighty hath given me life*" *(Job 33: 4)*. I am in awe of how very precise and definite the scripture is. The Father of Light is the only Creator of living beings and it is His very nature to impact light into each creature. This is the spiritual part of man that exists at the core of each being and remains at peace unperturbed by earthly circumstances.

The Inner Man and Christ in You

To make the confessions of Praise and Thanksgiving potent, the words need to come from the inner man that Peter the Apostle referred to as "*the hidden man of the heart*" *(1 Peter 3:4)*. Paul called it "*the Inner man*" *(Colossians 3:16);* "*Inward man*" *(2 Corinthians 4:16);* "*spirit of the mind*" *(Ephesians 4:23).*

The light sent at conception shows the point at which the spirit is imparted into the human body. The spirit man is where the Spirit of Christ lives within each human being. Many people do not recognize the fact that every man has a spirit and they confuse "the spirit" with the soul but look at these two verses.

> [8] **But there is a spirit in man**: and the inspiration of the Almighty giveth them understanding.
>
> *Job 32:8.*

> [23] *Now may God himself, the God of peace, make you pure, belonging only to him. **May your whole self— spirit, soul, and body**—be kept safe and without fault when our Lord Jesus Christ comes.*
>
> *1 Thessalonians 5:23 (NCV).*

These two verses show very cleary that there is indeed a spirit side to man. Within every physical person, there is a spirit that we cannot see with the physical eyes.

The act of being born-again popularly called *"giving your life to Christ"* or *"Getting Saved"* is the moment a transaction is made and a person makes the conscious effort to accept the lordship of Jesus over this inner man.

After salvation, Christ then begins a vital relationship with this inner man. Without this vital relationship, the sinful nature of Adam takes control. The Christ within creates within us pure images that blossom into manifestations of godliness. The Christ within stays with us even to the end when we die and the spirit returns to the Creator.

Looking at Paul's prayer, we cannot but notice that this knowledge of the inner man is one that was revealed to the early Apostles:

> *14 For this cause I bow my knees unto the Father of our Lord Jesus Christ,*
>
> *15 Of whom the whole family in heaven and earth is named,*
>
> *16 That he would grant you, according to the riches of his glory, to be strengthened with might by his Spirit in the inner man;*
>
> *17 That Christ may dwell in your hearts by faith; that ye, being rooted and grounded in love,*
>
> *18 May be able to comprehend with all saints what is the breadth, and length, and depth, and height;*

[19] And to know the love of Christ, which passeth knowledge, that ye might be filled with all the fulness of God.

Ephesians 3:14-19.

Even though the heart of man is desperately wicked and deceitful, there is a light inside us awaiting acceptance. Let us acknowledge and exalt the Christ within us which is our hope of glory.

PART II

CONFESSIONS FOR EVERYDAY LIVING

Chapter 6

Confessions on Praise and Thanksgiving to the Trinity

There is one body, and one Spirit, even as ye are called in one hope of your calling;

Ephesians 4:4

*G*eneralisation, sometimes, has at the root of it a lack of understanding of concepts or thoughts that underpin a particular area of discourse. For example, some like to stick with using "God" in statements because it means they can hide their true position on Jesus and the Holy Spirit behind the general title, "God".

Now, imagine how complicated our understanding of God would be if the seperation of personalities between Jesus, the Holy Spirit and God the Father, as is described in *John 14*, is not as clear as it is.

¹⁶ *And I will pray the Father, and he shall give you another*

Comforter, that he may abide with you for ever;

[17] *Even the Spirit of truth; whom the world cannot receive, because it seeth him not, neither knoweth him: but ye know him; for he dwelleth with you, and shall be in you.*

John 14:16-17.

Look at *verse 16* carefully. It says, "*I (Jesus)*" will pray "*the Father*"..."*another Comforter (The Holy Spirit: The Spirit of Truth).*" The three heavenly personalities are explained in this scripture.

I, personally, believe that, as Christians, we need to be more aware of this seperation and, therefore express our confessions to address the individual personalities in the Trinity, as outlined in this book.

Thanksgiving Confessions to the Father

Creator of the universe, the Great I AM THAT I AM, I acknowledge Your Power inside me as the source of my life; Your Breath as the sustainer of every single cell in my body; Your Light as my radiance; and Your Spirit in me as my all in all. I give thanks for Your Spirit as the life force within me. Forgive me for all the past misuse of my body which is your holy temple. Forgive me for misuse of my tongue which was created to exalt your holy name. Help me to honor you each day and to use your Spirit in me to live an enriched, purposeful, and wholesome life to the glory of your holy name.

Holy Spirit, help me to enter the gates of the Almighty God with thanksgiving, to proceed into His courts with praise, and to enter His Presence with grace and reverence.

- I am thankful that I am fearfully and wonderfully made.

- I am thankful that the LORD has broken the bands of my yoke and set me free.

- I am thankful that Jesus Christ brought redemption and sealed it with His blood.

- I am thankful that I am reconciled to God and adopted into the kingdom of light.

- I am thankful that I have been washed and made clean from all filthiness by the blood of the Lamb.

- I am thankful that I am not a servant anymore but a child of the Most High God.

- I am thankful that I am reigning with Christ in heavenly places, above principalities and powers of darkness.

- I am thankful that I have the authority to loose and bind.

- I am thankful that I am an heir according to the promise of God.

- I am thankful that the LORD always makes His strength perfect in my weaknesses.

- I am thankful that I can do all things through Christ who strengthens me.

- I am thankful that the LORD, daily, lifts up His countenance upon me and gives me peace.

- I am thankful that the LORD, daily, blesses me,

keeps me, makes His face to shine upon me, and is gracious unto me.

- I am thankful that the LORD, daily, satisfies my mouth with good things.

- I am thankful that I am redeemed from the curse of the law.

- I am thankful that I am a partaker of the inheritance of the Saints of Light.

- I am thankful that the LORD is gracious and merciful to me.

- I am thankful that I have been given access to come boldly to the Throne of Grace to obtain help in the hour of need.

- I am thankful that the LORD is my everlasting light and glory.

- I am thankful that the LORD crowns me daily with loving kindness and tender mercies.

- I am thankful that I have my name written in the Book of Life.

- I am thankful that I am destined for Eternal Life.

- I am aware that the LORD honors His promise to those who keep their feet from breaking the Sabbath and do not do as they please on the holy day, those who call the Sabbath a delight and make the LORD'S holy day honorable, and do not speak idle words. Such believers find joy in the LORD, who causes them to ride on the heights of the land and to feast on the inheritance of their father Jacob. *(Isaiah 58:13-14. NIV).*

- I am glad that the acceptable observance of the Sabbath comes with much blessings including good harvest, abundant provisions, deliverance, healing, victory, and full favor of our faithful God. *(Leviticus 26:2-13).*

Praise Confessions for "Christ in me"

"...Christ in you, the hope of glory:" (Colosians 1:27) Christ in me, my connection to the Almighty, I acknowledge you. My life–giving and inspiring streams of spiritual energy, I acknowledge you. The ever-present power of the Inner God in me, I acknowledge you. The Spirit that guides the progress of man out of material life into the spiritual I acknowledge you. The source of man's instinct and intuition, I acknowledge you. Fountain of man's noblest parts, I acknowledge you. The Flaming Star and Presence of Divine Love that shines within the lightless depth of every being, I acknowledge you. Christ in me the hope of glory, I acknowledge you. **Christ within is the eternal seal of truth!**

- Christ in me, the Uncreated Heaven-Born, be thou exalted.

- Christ in me, the mystery of all ages, be thou exalted.

- Christ in me, the boundless field of the unknown, be thou exalted.

- Christ in me, my Divine Infinite Mind, be thou exalted.

- Christ in me, the All-Knowing Presence, be thou exalted.

- Christ in me, the Still Small Voice, be thou exalted.

- Christ in me, the Fire that burns without scorching, be thou exalted.

- Christ in me, the Fire without flame, be thou exalted.

- Christ in me, the Electro-Spiritual Force, be thou exalted.

- Christ in me, the Effulgent Beam, be thou exalted.

- Christ in me, my Inner Sun, Inner God, and Inner Wisdom, be thou exalted.

- Christ in me, my Sun-lighted Peak of Wisdom and Illumination, be thou exalted.

- Christ, in me, the Heart of my Spiritual heart, be thou exalted.

- Christ, the Silent Force within me, be thou exalted.

- Christ, the Slayer of thought in me, be thou exalted.

- Christ in me, my Bridegroom who delights in me, be thou exalted.

- Christ in me, the Unutterable source of splendor, be thou exalted.

- Christ in me, the Unspeakably Beautiful Glory and Light, be thou exalted.

- Christ in me, the unthinkable source of bliss and peace, be thou exalted.

Praise Confessions for Jesus

- Rabboni, The Master Teacher of Galilee, our elder brother of light, the Lord of the Sabbath, be thou exalted.

- Sacred Head once wounded, scornfully surrounded with thorns, be thou exalted.

- Eternal Rock of glory, be thou exalted.

- My High Tower, my Strength, and Champion, be thou exalted.

- My Refuge, my Shelter, and Shield, be thou exalted.

- My Light, and my Shepherd be thou exalted.

- My Fortress and my Deliverer, be thou exalted.

- My Provider, my Inheritance, and Truth, be thou exalted

- The Branch from Jesse, the Root of David, be thou exalted.

- My Redeemer, the Horn of my salvation , be thou exalted.

- My Shepherd who tends his flock tenderly gathering the lambs in his arms, be thou exalted.

- Christ the everlasting Bread of Life, be thou exalted.

- Christ, the friend of sinners, be thou exalted.

- Christ our heavenly manna, be thou exalted.

- Christ the stricken Rock, be thou exalted.

- Christ the King Eternal, be thou exalted.

- Christ the fullness of God be thou exalted.

- Christ the fullness of all things, be thou exalted.

- Christ the Head of all principality and power be thou exalted.

- Christ the Corner-Stone, be thou exalted.

Thanksgiving Confessions for the Holy Spirit

- I am thanking the Holy Spirit for brooding over primordial chaos and giving it order. *(Genesis 1:2).*

- I am thanking the Holy Spirit for speaking through the prophets as recorded in the Old Testament and specifically for sending advance knowledge of the coming of the Savior through the prophet as written *(Isaiah 9:6-7).*

- I thank the Holy Spirit for the holy conception by Mary and also for making the Word flesh to dwell with man *(John 1:14).*

- I am thanking the Holy Spirit for enabling the Church on earth to obey the command to, "Go and teach all nations, baptizing them in the name of the Father, and of the Son, and of the Holy

Ghost." *(Mark 16:15; Matthew 28:19).*

- I am thanking the Holy Spirit that continues to speak through prophets today as of old. *(Luke 2:26; Luke 1:67)*

- I am thanking the Holy Spirit for the Spirit of adoption whereby we cry ABBA FATHER! *(Romans 8:15).*

- I am thankful that the Holy Spirit bears witness with my spirit that I am a child of the Living God. *(Romans 8:16; II Corinthians 6:18; John 1:12).*

- I am thanking the Holy Spirit for there is no condemnation to us who walk in the Spirit because the law of the Spirit in Christ Jesus hath made us free from the law of sin and death *(Romans 8:1-2).*

- I am thanking the Holy Spirit our Comforter sent by the Father *(John 14:16; John 15:26).*

- I am thanking the Holy Spirit who teaches us all things and brings all things to our remembrance *(I John 14:26).*

- I am thanking the Holy Spirit for interceding for us with deep groaning according to the will of God *(Romans 8:26-27).*

- I am thanking the Holy Spirit for the gifts of love, joy, peace, long-suffering, gentleness, goodness, faith, meekness, and temperance. *(Galatians 5:22-23).*

- I am thanking the Holy Spirit for being the Spirit of Truth that separates us from the world *(Romans 8:8, 9, 14, 16).*

- I am thanking the Holy Spirit that will lead us home to our Father at the end of our journey here on earth *(Romans 8:22-23)*

Praise Confessions to our Father

- I am praising the Great I AM THAT I AM, the Creator of heaven and earth who brings out the starry host one by one and calls them each by name.

- I am praising the Everlasting Father who has measured the waters in the hollow of His hand.

- I am praising the Almighty I AM who has marked off the heavens with His hands.

- I am daily praising the Rock of Ages who has held the dust of the earth in a bucket.

- I am daily enabled to sing a new song unto the Alpha and Omega who weighed the mountains on the scale and the hills in a balance.

- I am purposed to make His Omnipotent name to be remembered in all generations: to enable the people to praise the Great I AM forever and ever.

- I am praising the Creator who weighed the Islands as though they were fine dust.

- I am greatly praising the King of Ages before whom the nations are like a drop in a bucket.

- I am enabled to stand every morning to praise the Great I AM for His mighty power, mercy, and infinite wisdom.

- I am freely praising my Father and praising the

name of the only Living God, who sits enthroned above the circle of the earth, before whom the people of the earth are as grasshoppers.

- I am praising and rejoicing in the Mighty One and I am singing praise to the name of the Most High God.

- I am praising the Almighty Creator whose hands have made me and fashioned me.

- I am praising the Creator who causes the tender herbs to bud and spring forth.

- I am praising He who fills the appetite of tiny ants and feeds the birds, the lions and all animals He created.

- I am praising the Wisdom that gave the goodly wings unto the peacocks, strength unto horses and gave eagles instincts to mount up to great heights with eyes that behold afar off to seek her prey.

- I am praising the mighty God who made the behemoth *(land monster) and leviathan(sea monster)* with unimaginable force and abilities.

- I am praising my Eternal Father to pay what I have vowed.

- I am exalting and praising the Holy One of Israel for He has done wonderful things for me.

- I am exalting the Arm of the LORD that has lifted me up and has not made my foes to rejoice over me.

- I am praising the God who commands the morning and causes the dayspring to know its place.

- I am exalting the Controller of the treasures of snow, hail, rain and dew.

- I am exalting and giving thanks to the Wise Silence because of His righteousness and I will continue to sing praises to the name of THE LORD MOST HIGH.

- I am enabled to lift up my hands in the sanctuary and bless the LORD the Perceiver and Revealer of Truth.

Adoration and Worship Confessions

- I am worshipping the LORD my maker with all my heart as commanded.

- I am daily worshipping the I AM THAT I AM.

- I am daily worshipping the High and Lofty One that inhabits Eternity.

- I am daily worshipping the LORD OF HOST.

- I am daily worshipping my God, my Creator and Maker, and my King.

- I am daily worshipping my Eternal Rock, my Fortress, my High Tower, my Strength, my Light, and my Shield.

- I am assured that all the ends of the world shall remember and turn unto the LORD, and all the nations shall worship before Him.

- I am daily worshipping the LORD in the beauty of holiness and I fear before Him.

- I am worshipping Him that made heaven and earth,

the sea, and the fountains of waters.

- I am worshipping our Father who manifested our Lord Jesus Christ in the flesh, justified him in the spirit, in whom are hid all the treasures of wisdom and knowledge.

- I am worshipping our gracious and merciful Father who has given us the WORD through His Son.

- I am worshipping the Everlasting Father for the power in His WORD which is pure, unbounded, quick, sharp, and tried in fire seven times!

- I am worshipping my Provider who supplies all my needs.

- I am worshipping my Healer who heals all my infirmities.

- I am worshipping my Preserver who preserves my going out and my coming in.

- I am worshipping my faithful Creator who rejoices over me to do me good.

- I am worshipping my God of war who breaks the bow of my enemies and cuts their spear asunder.

- I am worshipping my God the Consuming Fire who burns the chariots of my enemies in the fire.

- I am worshipping the God who laid the foundation of the earth and the heavens are the work of His hands.

- I am worshipping the God who stretched out the land over an empty space and hangs the earth upon nothing.

- I am worshipping the God who compassed the waters with bounds, until the day and night came to an end.

- I am worshipping the God who shut up the sea with doors and gave a decree that the waters should not pass His commandments.

- I am worshipping the God who made a way for the lightning and thunder and divided a watercourse for the overflowing of water.

- I am worshipping the God who knows the ordinances of heaven and sets the dominion on the earth.

- I am worshipping the God who appointed the moon for seasons and makes the sun to know it's going down.

- I am worshipping the God who upholds all things by the Word of His power and the power of His Word.

- I am worshipping the God who is able to bring water out of a rock.

- I am worshipping the God who is able to turn the dry land into water springs.

- I am worshipping the God who is able to make a barren woman be a joyful mother of children.

- I am worshipping our Father of light, who has immortality dwelling in the light which no man can approach.

- I am worshipping the God who is clothed with glory and majesty in whose hands are riches and honor.

- I am daily praising, exalting, and honoring the King of Heaven, whose works are truth and His ways judgment.

- I am worshipping my dwelling place in all generations.

Our Heavenly Father, the Omnipotent and eternal I AM THAT I AM, the Blessed and only Potentate, the invincible and invisible One who dwells in unapproachable light, be thou glorified. The Lord of hosts, who is wonderful in counsel and excellent in working, be thou glorified. Be thou exalted O God, above the heaven: and thy glory above all the earth.

> [11] *Thine, O Lord is the greatness, and the power, and the glory, and the victory, and the majesty: for all that is in the heaven and in the earth is thine; thine is the kingdom, O Lord, and thou art exalted as head above all.*
>
> *1 Chronicles 29:11.*

> [24] *To him who is able to keep you from stumbling and to present you before his glorious presence without fault and with great joy—*
>
> [25] *to the only God our Savior be glory, majesty, power and authority, through Jesus Christ our Lord, before all ages, now and forevermore! Amen.*
>
> *Jude 24-25 (NIV).*

Chapter 7

Confessions Regarding
Our Identity in Christ

*...be mindful of the words which were spoken before by
the holy prophets, and of the commandment of us the
apostles of the Lord and Saviour:*

2 Peter 3:2

*A*s you explore these confessions, it is
important to remember that the Bible says
you can make confessions unto salvation. I will
encourage you to make these confessions as you
believe for the manifestation of divine power, good
health, abundant life, full joy, perfect peace, and
wisdom.

We should enter into this practice of daily confessions
in the full realization that God's Word is powerful,
sharper than any two-edged sword, and capable of
pulling down strongholds. The word of God is able
to cast down imaginations and bring every thought
to the obedience of Christ.

We celebrate the fact that the Word is forever settled in heaven and will accomplish that for which it was sent. We shoud have unshakable faith that as we commit to daily confessions of the Word and obey God's laws to love, we, assuredly, will reap adundant rewards. Our identity with Christ is the foundation of our faith and hope.

Confessions on My Christian Identity

- I am in Christ, I am a new creature, old things are passed away, all things become new. *(II Corinthians 5:17)*

- I have been delivered from the power of darkness, I have been translated into the Kingdom of His dear Son. *(Colossians 1:13)*

- I am redeemed from the curse of the law. *(Galatians 3:13)*

- I am a child of the God that created heaven and earth and hangs the earth upon nothing, the God that sealed the sea with doors and ordained stars and moons. *(Proverbs 8:29; Psalm 8:3)*

- I am a child of the Living God, and the Holy Spirit bears witness of this fact. *(Romans 8:16; II Corinthians 6:18; John 1:12)*

- I cry, "Abba, Father" by the Spirit of adoption in me. *(Romans 8:15)*

- I am a branch abiding in the vine and bringing forth much fruit. *(John 15:5-6)*

- I am a royal priesthood created to show forth the

praises of my God and Creator who has called me out of darkness into His marvelous Light. *(I Peter 2:9; Isaiah 9:2; Isaiah 43:21; Colossians 1:13)*

- I am a tabernacle that is not made with hands. *(Hebrews 9:11; Acts 17:24)*

- I am the image and likeness of the Living God. *(Genesis 1:27)*

- I am an heir of the Father; I am a joint heir with the Son. *(Romans 8:16-17)*

- I am of the household of God, I am an heir of the Kingdom of God. *(James 2:5)*

- I am saved and made whole through grace. *(Ephesians 2:5)*

- I am inhabited by the same creative Spirit that hovered on the face of the waters at creation and gave the earth order. *(Genesis 1:2)*

- I am inhabited by the spirit that raised Christ from the dead. *(Romans 8:11)*

- I am a part of everything that God created and declared "very good". *(Genesis 1:31)*

- I am a child of the Father of Light, I am light in the Earth. *(Matthew 5:14)*

- I am in awe that Jesus said, the kingdom of God is within me. *(Luke 17:21)*.

- I am grateful for the gift of the Holy Spirit and the kingdom of God that exists with power within me. *(Acts 1:8)*.

- I am awake to the truth of who I am as a healthy, whole, perfect emanation of God, for in Christ I live, move, and have my being. *(Acts 17:28).*

- I am awake to the power that I received and the presence of God working through me. *(Acts 1:8).*

- I am a spiritual being, unlimited, unfettered, unstoppable, and with full dominion. *(Psalm 8:4-8).*

- I am awake to the Indwelling Divine Potential in me that strengthens me and enables me to do all things. *(Philippians 4:13).*

- I am comforted that the LORD takes hold of my hand each day and says to me, "Do not fear, I will help you". *(Isaiah 41:13) (NIV).*

- I am assured that from everlasting to everlasting, the LORD'S love is with those who fear Him and His righteousness with their children's children. *(Psalm 103:17).*

- I am encouraged to praise God who holds back His wrath for His name sake and for the sake of those who praise Him. *(Isaiah 48:9).*

- I am assured that goodness and mercy shall follow me all the days of my life. *(Psalm 23:6).*

- I am assured that God's mercy is with them that fear him from generation to generation. *(Luke 1:50).*

- I am filled with the wonder-working power of God. *(John 1:12).*

- I am Christ's ambassador through whom God makes His appeal to mankind and I am set apart by the Father and sent into the World to spread the Word. *(II Corinthians 5:20; John 10:34).*

- I am the living expression of God's perfect creation, a perfect expression of wholeness. *(Psalm 139:14).*

- I am called and chosen. *(Matthew 22:14; Isaiah 42:6).*

- I am called according to His purpose, I am justified and glorified. *(Romans 8:30).*

- I am a vessel unto honor. *(Romans 9:21).*

- I am redeemed from the curses of labor pains, inordinate affection, and hard labor. *(Genesis 3:16-17; Galatians 3:13).*

- I am not under law but I am under grace; sin shall therefore not have dominion over me. *(Romans 6:14).*

- I am more than a conqueror through Christ who loves me. *(Romans 8:37).*

- I am made to be a priest and serve God and I am destined to reign with Christ on earth. *(Revelation 5:10).*

- I am in the realm of all possibilities in Christ for with God all things are possible *(Mark 9:23, Luke 1:37).*

- I am always hopeful in Christ. *(Romans 5:5).*

- I am clothed by grace with the righteousness of Christ. *(Romans 5:21).*

- I am blessed to be fruitful, to multiply, to fill the earth, to subdue it, and to have dominion. *(Genesis*

1:28).

- I am graven upon the palms of the Most High God. *(Isaiah 49:16).*

- I am given the power to know the mysteries of the kingdom of heaven. *(Matthew 13:11).*

- I am assured that the Spirit of God goes ahead of me and removes obstacles. *(Isaiah 40:4; Psalm 5:8).*

- I am under the law of life in Christ which has freed me from the law of sin and death. *(Romans 8:1).*

- I am enabled by the Holy Spirit to triumph in Christ in every place. *(II Corinthians 2:14).*

- I am wholly surrendered to the Holy Spirit and I am free from condemnation and the law of sin and death. *(Romans 8:1).*

- I am open to the inspirations of the Holy Spirit and I therefore, have the capacity to live freely and fully. *(Romans 8:9).*

- I am the joy of the Spirit of Christ in expression. *(Romans 15:13).*

- I am wise with the wisdom of the Holy Spirit. *(Proverbs 2:10-12).*

- I am enriched by gifts of the Spirit. *(Galatians 6:8).*

- I am attuned to the Holy Spirit and act on guidance I receive. *(Romans 8:14).*

- I am comforted that nothing can separate me from the love of God. *(Romans 8:35).*

- I am never alone because I have the Indwelling Christ in me, my hope of glory. (*Colossians 1:27).*

- I am enabled by the Holy Spirit to show unto this generation the power of God. *(Psalm 71:18).*

- I am like a watered garden and like a spring of water that never dries. *(Isaiah 58:11).*

- I am exuberant, fueled, and propelled by irrepressible joy! *(Isaiah 55:12).*

- I am in awe of Earth's bountiful blessings. *(Psalm 19:1-2).*

- I am grateful for blessings manifested and all those yet to be. *(John 4:35).*

- I am divinely guided to my greatest happiness and success. *(Proverbs 4:11-12).*

- I am tranquil as I experience love, peace, and joy within me. *(Philippians 4:4-7).*

- I am rejoicing daily and propelled by my joyful hope in Christ. *(Hebrew 3:18; I Thessalonians 5:6).*

- I daily rejoice in the LORD God of my salvation (Hebrew 3:18; Isaiah 61:10).

- I am rejoicing daily in the Holy One of Israel. *(Isaiah 41:16b Philippians 3:1; Philippians 4:4)*

- I am empowered to keep rejoicing daily as I release hurts and disappointments from my soul. *(Psalm 149:2; Ecclesiastics 2:10).*

- I am daily trusting in divine order to unfold in my favor with efficiency and perfect timing. *(Psalm 69:13; Isaiah 49:8).*

Chapter 8

Confessions on my Daily Benefits in Christ

...The stone which the builders rejected is become the head of the corner:

Mark 12:10

- I daily present my body as a living sacrifice to God as commanded. *(Romans 12:1; Psalm 51:2,10)*

- I daily present my will, thoughts and actions to the Holy Spirit for cleansing and illumination. *(Romans 12:1)*

- I am energized daily in silent prayer and meditation as I become still to tap into the Power within me. *(Psalm 46:10).*

- I am anointed with fresh oil daily. *(Psalm 92:10; Psalm 23:5).*

- I am renewed daily in mind, body, and spirit. *(II Corinthians 4:16).*

- I am empowered each day by the Holy Spirit. *(Acts 1:8).*

- I am being blessed and multiplied every day. *(Hebrews 6:13-14).*

- I daily affirm both wisdom and wealth as God-ordained forms of shelter and defense for me. *(Proverbs 2:10-12; Ecclesiastes 10:19).*

- I am guided daily to walk circumspectly to redeem the time and be wise because the days are evil. *(Ephesians 5:16).*

- I daily shout 'Hallelujah' and the walls of obstruction and delay are collapsing daily. *(Joshua 6:20; Revelations 19:1, 3, 4, 6).*

- I am transformed daily by the renewing of my mind. *(Romans 12:2).*

- I daily acknowledge God in all my ways and I am always directed aright. *(Psalm 37:5; Proverbs 3:6).*

- I trust the LORD daily with my whole heart as commanded. *(Proverbs 3:5).*

- I am energized daily by the Spirit within me and I channel my energy into joyful activities. *(Habakkuk 3:18-19).*

- I daily walk in faith and not by sight. *(II Corinthians 5:7).*

- I am guided daily by the still small voice within. *(I King 19:12; Isaiah 30:21).*

- I am quickened daily by the spirit that raised Christ

from the dead, which also dwells in me. *(Romans 8:11).*

- I am awake to the Christ within me, the hope of glory. *(Colossians 1:27).*

- I daily conform to the image of Christ. *(Romans 8:29).*

- I daily lean on a Rock that is higher than me and I am secure. *(Psalm 61:2)*

- I am complete in Him who is the head of all principality and power. *(Colossians 2:10).*

- I am daily shielded by His banner over me which is LOVE. *(Song of Solomon 2:4).*

- I daily feed on the Bread of Life and drink of the Living Fountain. *(John 6:35).*

- I am a courageous conqueror as I put on my spiritual armor daily to quench the darts of the enemy. *(Ephesians 6:11).*

- I daily make wise choices and make good judgments as led by the Holy Spirit and I am soaring high as an eagle. *(John 14:26; Luke 12:12; Isaiah 40:31).*

- I am greeting each new day with positive expectancy as I affirm the goodness of God. *(Psalm 118:24).*

- I expect miracles every day and my needs are turning into miracles daily. *(Psalm 118:14-15).*

- I perform acts of kindness that will enable my light to break forth like the dawn. *(Isaiah 58:7-8).*

- I am in communion with God daily through His Word. *(John 15:7).*

- I daily commit my cause to God who does great, marvelous, and unsearchable things without number for me. *(Job 5:9)*

- I am humbled that God so loved the world that He gave His Beloved Son to redeem us so that whoever believes in Him shall not perish but have eternal life. (John 3:16).

- I am delighted that those who keep the Sabbath will be given an everlasting name that will not be cut off. (Isaiah 56:4-5).

Chapter 9

Confessions on Protection

...And it shall come to pass, that before they call, I will answer; and while they are yet speaking, I will hear.:

Isaiah 65:24

- I am dwelling in the secret place of the Most High. *(Psalm 91:1).*

- I am abiding under the shadow of the Almighty. *(Psalm 91:1).*

- I am not afraid of the arrow that flies by day. *(Psalm 91:5).*

- I am not afraid of the pestilence that walks in darkness. *(Psalm 91:6).*

- I am not afraid of noonday dangers and destructions. *(Psalm 91:6).*

- I dwell in a peaceful and secure habitation. *(Isaiah 32:18).*

- I am not afraid of the roaring lion; I am not

disturbed by its noise. *(Isaiah 31:4).*

- I am delivered from the hand of the wicked and I am redeemed from the grip of the terrible. *(Jeremiah 15:21).*

- I am strengthened, helped, and upheld by the right hand of the Almighty. *(Isaiah 41:10).*

- I am created to live my life in freedom from fear, revenge, and malice. Therefore, every opportunity for accusation from the enemy is closed down. *(Ephesians 4:31-32).*

- I am in Christ and my life is hidden with Christ in God. *(Colossians 3:3; John 14:20).*

- I am delivered from the fear of the oppressor. *(Isaiah 49:25-26).*

- I am assured that the LORD will contend with those who contend with me. *(Isaiah 49:25).*

- I am more than a conqueror through Christ who loves me. *(Romans 8:37).*

- I obtain mercy and find grace daily to help in time of need. *(Hebrews 4:16).*

- I am hidden in His pavilion, in the secret place of His tabernacle. *(Psalm 27:5).*

- I am lifted up above my enemies round about me. *(Psalm 27:6).*

- I am strong and of good courage, as commanded by the LORD. *(Joshua 1:6).*

- I am not afraid or dismayed because the LORD is

with me wherever I go. *(Joshua 1:9)*.

- I am doing all things through Christ who strengthens me. *(Philippians 4:13)*.

- I am assured that as it is written, all who seek my life will be disgraced and put to shame *(Psalm 35:4)*.

- I am protected from the scourge of the tongue *(Job 5:21)*.

- I am kept secretly in a pavilion from the strife of tongues. *(Psalm 31:20)*

- I am redeemed from death and the power of the sword. *(Job 5:20)*.

- I am assured that all weapons created to make war with me shall not prosper and my accusers will be refuted *(Isaiah 54:17)*.

- I have the power to tread upon my enemies who shall be ashes under the soles of my feet. *(Malachi 4:3)*.

- I am encouraged to use the heavenly army to battle on my behalf daily because they were created to be our weapons of war. *(Jeremiah 51:20)*

- I am daily running into the name of the I AM THAT I AM which is a strong tower that keeps me safe *(Proverbs 18:10)*.

Night Protection

- I am assured that as I shall lie down to sleep, no one will make me afraid and my sleep shall be sweet *(Job 11:18-19; Proverbs 3:24)*.

- I am assured that the angels of God encamp around my habitation to protect me while I sleep. *(Psalm 34:7).*

- I am daily accepting the blessings of God upon my habitation and God's peace and harmony prevails within my walls *(Psalm 122:7).*

- I am assured that the LORD keeps me from all harm and watches over my life. *(Psalm 121:2).*

- I am assured that the LORD makes me dwell in safety. *(Psalm 4:8).*

- I am watched by the LORD's angels who have been commanded to encamp around me to guard and deliver me even while I sleep.*(Psalm 91:11; Psalm 34:7).*

- I am enabled to rise at midnight and give thanks to the LORD my God *(Psalm 119:62).*

Chapter 10

Confessions on Obedience

If ye be willing and obedient, ye shall eat the good of the land::

Isaiah 1:19

- I am encouraged to be obedient by the Word which says: "If ye be willing and obedient, ye shall eat of the good of the land". *(Isaiah 1:19) (KJV).*

- I am purposed to obey God's commands and to do those things that are pleasing in His sight. *(I John 3:22).*

- I am comforted that as by one man's disobedience many were made sinners, so by the obedience of one shall many be made righteous. *(Romans 5:19).*

- I am obligated to honor the sabbath which God revealed to be a sign between God and man for the generations to come *(Exodus 31:13) (NIV)*. And to reverence the laws inscribed by the finger of God. *(Exodus 31:15,18) (NIV).*

- I am declaring that the Sabbath which is mentioned 126 times in the Old Testament and 62 times in the New Testament is worthy of our attention and obedience. *(Author's note).*

- I am bound as a believer to follow the example of Jesus, the author, and finisher of our faith, who always worshipped on the Sabbath as was his custom. *(Luke 4:16).*

- I am certain that the Scriptures make it very explicit that Sunday is the first day of the week and in obedience to the scriptures, this day should not be changed. *(Luke 24:1; John 20:1, 19; Mark 16:1-2, 9; Matthew 28:1; Acts 20:7).*

- I am warned against "the man doomed to destruction. who will oppose and exalt himself over everything that is called God, who is worshipped, so that he sets himself up in God's temple, proclaiming himself to be God." *(II Thessalonians 2:4) (NIV).*

- I am comforted that those who obey the laws of God and had not worshiped the beast, neither his image, neither had received his mark upon their foreheads or in their hands, shall live and reign with Christ a thousand years. *(Revelations 20:4) (KJV).*

- I am joyful that it is written that anyone who obeys the fourth commandment by keeping the Sabbath without desecrating it will be blessed. *(Isaiah 56:2) (NIV).*

Chapter 11

Confessions on Light and Healing

But he was wounded for our transgressions, he was bruised for our iniquities: the chastisement of our peace was upon him; and with his stripes we are healed:

Isaiah 53:5

- I am confident that my inward spirit is renewed day by day by the Holy Spirit. *(II Corinthians 4:16).*

- I am daily accepting the supremacy of my Creator in (the 60 trillion) cells of my body because all the parts of my body are written in His book. *(Psalm 139:16).*

- I am healed of broken heart and wounds by the Holy Spirit. *(Psalm 147:3).*

- I am a perfect expression of divine wholeness *(Colossians 2:9; Ephesians 4:13).*

- I am healed by his stripes, for my iniquity was laid upon Him. *(Isaiah 53:5).*

- I am healed of all diseases including anxiety, fear and addiction. *(Psalm 103:3).*

- I am assured that the LORD daily makes His face shine upon me. *(Numbers 6:25).*

- I am soaked in the glorious light of the Holy Spirit everyday. *Ezekiel 36:27.*

- I am assisted by the Holy Spirit to gird my loins and keep my light burning everyday. *(Luke 12:35)*

- I am radiating light everywhere I go because of the light of God in me. *Matthew 5:16*

- I am guided by the light of God which is a lamp unto my feet and light unto my path. *(Psalm 119:105).*

- I am daily co-creating with my Father because I open my heart and mind to His light through the Word. *(Psalm 119:130; John 10:34).*

- I am claiming the Father's blessings every day for my future and so be it: "The LORD bless thee, and keep thee. The LORD make His face to shine upon thee and be gracious unto thee. The LORD lift up His countenance upon thee, and give thee peace". *(Numbers 6:24-26).*

12

Confessions for your Future

For I know the thoughts that I think toward you, saith the Lord, thoughts of peace, and not of evil, to give you an expected end:

Jeremiah 29:11

- I am affirming with strong faith that every false prophecy over my future will come to naught and every plan that is not of God will dissolve and dissipate to be replaced by the divine will of God for me and my offspring. *(Numbers 23:8, 23; Matthews 15:13).*

- I am confident that my future has great and glorious potential. *(Romans 15:3).*

- I am not getting fulfillment from past successes and I am not bound by past failures, but I am propelled by my joyful hope in Christ. *(Habakkuk 3:18).*

- I am assured that my descendants shall be many and my offspring like the grass of the earth. *(Job 5:25).*

- I am daily pleading that the LORD should deal with me bountifully so that I may live to keep His word. *(Psalm 119:17).*

- I am trusting in the LORD to remove reproach and contempt from me to enable me to shine for His praise and glory *(Psalm 119:22)*

- I am assured that my seed shall be taught of the LORD and shall be great. *(Isaiah 54:13).*

- I am assured that as it is written, I, and the children the LORD has given me, are for signs and wonders. *(Isaiah 8:18).*

- I am assured that my sons shall be as plants in a watered garden and my daughters as polished cornerstones. *(Psalm 144:12).*

- I am looking beyond the appearance of lack, I am focusing on God as the ever-present, never-failing source of my supplies. *(Philippians 4:19).*

- I am able to reach any goal, accomplish any task and succeed in every area of my life by the power of the Holy Spirit *(Revelations 3:8; Isaiah 60:1)*

- I am assured that I shall not die young. I shall live to declare the works of the LORD. *(Psalm 118:17)*

- I am claiming my good through developing and using the God-given qualities that are within me. *(I Timothy 4:14; II Timothy 1:6).*

- I am assured that the Lord will do me good at my latter end. *(Job 8:7, 42:12; Deuteronomy 8:16).*

- I am assured that as it is commanded and written,

my children will honor me. *(Exodus 20:12; Luke 18:20)*.

- I am assured that I shall come to the grave at a full age. *(Job 5:26)*.

- I am assured and preserved to see the goodness of God in the land of the living. *(Psalm 27:13)*.

- I am progressing in the strength of the Lord God; who brought me out of my mother's womb. *(Psalm 71:6-7)*.

- I am assured that my family is blessed, my children shall surround my table, and I shall see my children's children. *(Psalm 127:3-4, 128:3-6, 144:12; Proverbs 17:6)*.

Confessions on Success

- I am preparing adequately each day to scale over problems and obstacles with the Word and power of God. (Joshua 1:11).

- I am equipped by the Word of God to take dominion and to succeed. (Psalm 8:6).

- I am crowned with glory and honor by my Creator. (Psalm 8:5).

- I am claiming my dreams and visions for manifestation to show the glory of God. (Isaiah 43:7).

- I am getting wisdom and understanding from the Word of God that will secure my success. (Proverbs 4:5).

- I am one with the Big Mind, the God of Impossibilities that has a solution to all problems, therefore, I cannot fail. (Luke 1:37; 18:27).

- I am delighted that the LORD wishes above all things that I may prosper and be in good health. (3 John 2).

- I am established to be the head and never the tail. (Deuteronomy 28:13).

- I am meditating on the Word of God and confessing the promises of God to make my life prosperous and successful. (Joshua 1:8).

- I am asking for and being blessed with wisdom and understanding every day as I meditate on the Word of God. (James 1:5).

- I am not afraid or dismayed because I know that the LORD is always with me to give me victory and success. (Joshua 1:9).

- I am destined to succeed and be great and be a wonder on this earth. (Isaiah 8:18).

- I am standing in the anointing power of the Most High and I decree that I have more understanding than all my teachers. (Psalm 119:99).

- I am shining like a star because my light has come and the glory of God is risen upon me. (Isaiah 60:1).

PART III

Topical Confessions

Chapter 13

Topical Confessions

Is not my word like as a fire? saith the Lord; and like a
hammer that breaketh the rock in pieces?

Jeremiah 23:29

Confessions on Anger

- I am a child of a forgiving God who is gracious, compassionate, slow to anger, and abounding in love and great mercy. *(Psalm 145:8).*

- I am enabled to rid myself of the things that God hates such as anger, rage, malice, slander, and filthy language. *(Colossians 3:8; Ephesians 4:31-32).*

- I am enabled to resolve issues and get rid of any anger before sundown. *(Ephesians 4:26).*

- I am realizing that anger gives the devil a chance to play havoc in my life. *(Ephesians 4:27).*

- I am admonished that, "A man of wrath stirs up strife, and a man given to anger commits much transgression." *(Proverbs 29:22)*.

- I am learning to be quick to listen, slow to speak, and slow to become angry. *(James 1:19)*.

- I am made to understand that man's anger does not promote the righteousness of God. *(James 1:20)*.

- I am to remember that a wise man never argues with a fool knowing that silence is the best answer for a fool who may stir up anger if given audience. *(Proverbs 29:9)*.

- I am certain that it is better to dwell in the wilderness than with a contentious and angry person. *(Proverbs 21:19)*

- I am warned that wrath is cruel and anger is outrageous. *(Proverbs 27: 4)*.

- I am praying to be quick to listen, slow to speak and slow to become angry. *(James 1:19)*.

Confessions on Fear

- I am rolling away the stone of anxiety and fear; I am filled with hope and joyful expectations. *(Matthews 6:28-34)*.

- I am not afraid because God is my refuge and strength and my ever-present help in trouble. *(Hebrews 13:6; Psalm 46:1)*.

- I am not afraid of sudden disaster that overtakes the wicked because the LORD will keep my feet from being snared. *(Proverbs 3:25-26)*.

- I am rescued from the hand of the enemy and

enabled to serve God without fear. *(Luke 1:74)*.

- I am holding on to God's promise which says " And I will give them one heart, and one way, that they fear me for ever , for the good of them and of their children after them". *(Jeremiah 32:39)*.

- I am delighted that the Most High promised to make an everlasting covenant with us and to put His fear in our hearts. *(Jeremiah 32:40)*.

- I am grateful that God has not given me a spirit of fear but has given me a Spirit of power, love and of a sound mind. *(2 Timothy 1:7)*.

- I am happy that I have not received the spirit of bondage to fear but I have received the Spirit of adoption whereby I am able to cry "Abba Father". *(Romans 8:15)*.

- I am filled with faith and shall not be afraid of the terror by night nor the arrow that flies by day nor the pestilence that walks in darkness nor the destruction at noonday. *(Psalm 91: 4-6)*

- I am daily affirming the written promise "fear not for thou shall not be ashamed neither be confounded for thou shall not be put to shame." *(Isaiah 54:4)*

- I am declaring with boldness that the LORD is my helper and shield and I shall not fear what man can do unto me. *(Hebrew 13:6)*.

Confessions on Giving

- I am enabled to tithe and to give offerings so that I may increase and prosper. *(Deuteronomy 14:22, 29)*.

- I am giving seed-faith of my time, money, and love and I am receiving a good return of all I give. *(Luke 6:38)*.

- I am receiving good measure, pressed down, shaken together, and running over as my reward for giving. *(Luke 6:38)*.

- I am like a tree planted by the rivers of water that brings forth its fruit in season. *(Psalm 1:3)*.

- I am like a spring of water whose waters fail not. *(Isaiah 58:11)*.

- I am blessed with every herb that yields seed and every tree whose fruit yields seed. *(Genesis 1:29)*.

- I am given bread daily and my water is sure. *(Isaiah 33:16)*.

- I am blessed with the treasures and the hidden riches of secret places. *(Isaiah 45:3)*.

- I am blessed and lending unto many and will never borrow. *(Deuteronomy 28:12)*.

- I am established as a head and I am never the tail. *(Deuteronomy 28:13)*.

- I am blessed when I come in and I am blessed when I go out. *(Deuteronomy 28:6)*.

- I am blessed in the City and blessed in the field. *(Deuteronomy 28:3)*.

- I am sucking the abundance of the sea and blessed with treasures hid in the sand. *(Deuteronomy 33:19).*

- I am encouraged that it is written that those who keep the Sabbath without desecrating it will be brought to God's holy mountain and given joy in God's house of prayer. *(Isaiah 56:6-7 NIV).*

- I am making my requests known by prayer, supplication, and thanksgiving and I am blessed. *(Philippians 4:6).*

- I am self-sufficient in all things and I have an abundance for every charitable work through the grace of God. *(II Corinthians 9:8).*

- I am a magnet to health, wealth, love, and prosperity. *(Psalm 23:6).*

- I am daily acknowledging God as the source of my total supply. *(James 1:17).*

- I am prospering spiritually and financially and I am in good health. *(III John 2).*

- I am receiving the supply to all my needs according to His riches in glory by Christ. *(Philippians 4:19).*

- I am affirming both wisdom and money are gifts that come directly from God. *(Colossians 2:3; I King 4:29).*

- I affirm daily both wisdom and money as God-ordained forms of defense for me. *(Ecclesiastes 7:12).*

- I am looking beyond the appearance of lack, I am focusing on God as the ever-present, never- failing source of my needs. *(Psalm 23:1, 121:1-2)*.

- I am daily lifting my eyes unto the hills from whence cometh my help. *(Psalm 23:1)*.

- I am rich through the grace of our Lord Jesus Christ who was rich but became poor so that I, through His poverty, might become rich. *(I Corinthians 8:9)*.

- I am assured that money which is mine by divine right is reaching me in perfect ways. *(I Corinthians 9:8)*.

Confessions on Honesty

- I am purposed to work honestly and to be of honest report. *(Acts 6:3)*.

- I am dwelling on things that are true and honest. *(Philippians 14:8)*.

- I am purposed to be careful to do right, not only in the sight of the Lord but also in the sight of people. *(II Corinthians 8:21)*.

- I am enabled to reject gain from extortion and I am keeping my hand from accepting bribes. *(Isaiah 33:15)*.

- I am purposed not to withhold good from those who deserve it and not to take advantage of or oppress anyone. *(Proverbs 3:27; Leviticus 25:17)*.

- I am admonished not to be a witness against my neighbours without cause and not to deceive anyone with my lips. *(Proverbs 24: 28)*

- I am warned that a false witness shall be punished

and he that speaks lies will not escape punishment. *(Proverbs 19:5)*.

- I am purposed to tell the truth always in the name of the LORD. *(I Kings22:16)*.

- I am attesting to the faithfulness of God to establish those who are honest and truthful. *(Proverbs 12:19)*.

- I am praying daily to be conformed to the image of Christ and to be honest in all my ways as required of a child of God. *(Romans 13:13)*.

Confessions on Hope

- I am assured that Christ in me is my hope of glory. *(Colossians 1:27)*.

- I am daily strengthened and given courage by my hope in the LORD, my Maker. *(Psalm 31:24)*

- I am receiving hope daily from my God who is the health of my countenance. *(Psalm 42: 11)*.

- I am daily putting my hope in the Lord God who has been my trust from my youth. *(Psalm 71: 5)*.

- I am rejoicing in the hope that is laid up for me in heaven as a believer. *(Colossians 1:5)*.

- I am begotten into a lively hope by the resurrection of Jesus from the dead. *(I Peter: 3)*.

- I am being uplifted by my hope in Christ. *(I John 3:3)*.

- I am happy because I have the God of Jacob for my help and my hope is in the LORD my God. *(Psalm*

146: 5).

- I am filled with joy and peace and abounding in hope by the power of the Holy Spirit. *(Romans 15:13).*

- I am admonished to glory in tribulation knowing that tribulation increases patience and patience enhances experience and experience gives us hope and hope never makes one ashamed. *(Romans 5:3-5).*

- I am assured that the LORD will always hear me when I call because all my hope is in the LORD my God. *(Psalm 38: 15).*

- I am looking for the blessed hope of the glorious appearing of our Savior Jesus Christ. *(Titus 2:13).*

Confessions on Humility

- I am weary of the reward of a proud heart which is estrangement from the presence of God. *(Psalm 138:6).*

- I am warned that Lucifer fell because of pride. Lucifer said in his heart that he will ascend into heaven, exalt his throne above the stars of God and be like the Most High. *(Isaiah 14:12-15).*

- I am praying for the anointing of the Holy Spirit that will make me humble in spirit and in my heart because God searches the heart of man. *(I Samuel 16: 7).*

- I am praying for a humble spirit because this is the gift that trumps other requirements for spiritual growth. *(Psalm 149:4; Psalm 138:6).*

Confessions on Joy

- I am worshiping God in the spirit and rejoicing in Christ daily. *(Philippians 3:3).*

- I am rejoicing in the shadow of the wings of my God and Creator. *(Psalm 63:7).*

- I am rejoicing in the LORD greatly always. *(Philippians 4:4).*

- I am drawing water out of the wells of salvation with joy. *(Isaiah 12:3).*

- I am eternal excellence; I am the joy of many generations. *(Isaiah 60:15).*

- I am the joy of the Spirit of Christ in expression. *(Romans 15:13)*

- I am daily rejoicing in my salvation which has opened my earthen vessel to receive the flow of the living presence of the Most High God. *(II Corinthians 4:7)*

- I am daily rejoicing in the Holy Spirit that enables me to partake of the wondrous life in the Spirit realm and enjoy the light of God's presence. *(Psalm 116:17; Genesis 3: 2-6; I John 1:7)*

- I am enabled by the Holy Spirit to be joyful in tribulations knowing that trials are like physical exercises that strengthen my spiritual muscles and mold me for the Master's use. *(II Corinthians 4:17; Psalm 27:14; Romans 5:3).*

- I am joyful that it is not by power or by might but that all things are made possible by the Spirit of the Most High. *(Zecharia4:6; Isaiah 30:17).*

- I am called into a life of constant communion with my Creator, and to be joyful in my King the source of my joy. *(Psalm 149: 2).*

- I am exhorted to "rejoice evermore" in the Lord always having been appointed to obtain salvation by our Lord Jesus Christ. *(I Thessalonians 5: 9, Philippians 4;4 ; psalm 9 14).*

- I am overflowing with joy from a heart where God has poured His peace like a river *(Isaiah 66 ;12-14).*

- I am joyful that I am planted as a noble vine and a whole seed. *(Jeremiah 2:21).*

- I am rejoicing in the LORD, my soul is joyful in my God for He has clothed me with the garments of salvation and has covered me with the robe of righteousness *(Isaiah 61:10).*

- I am admonished to go out with joy each day and to be led forth with peace. *(Isaiah 55:12).*

- I am appointed to rejoice in the name of the Most High. *(Psalm 89: 16).*

- I am assured that the voice of rejoicing shall fill my tabernacle as a child of the Living God. *(Psalm 118:15).*

- I am certain that my portion is to rejoice and to give thanks at the remembrance of the holiness of the Most High. *(Psalm 97:11-12).*

- I am rejoicing daily with joy unspeakable for the gift of salvation and of the Spirit. *(I Peter 1:8).*

- I am rejoicing in the LORD the Commander of the armies of Israel who commands the wind to carry away my enemies and the whirlwind to scatter them. *(Isaiah 41:16).*

- I am certain that the joy of the LORD is my strength always. *(Nehemiah 8:10).*

Confessions on Mercy

- I am daily acknowledging God as "The LORD, The LORD God, merciful and gracious, longsuffering, and abundant in goodness and truth". *(Exodus 34: 6).*

- I am pleading daily for the mercy of the LORD for it is not of him who wills nor of him who runs, but of God who shows mercy on whom He pleases. *(Romans 9:15).*

- I am assured that the LORD's mercy is everlasting. *(Psalm 100:5; Luke 6:36).*

- I am trusting in the merciful kindness of my Creator. *(Psalm 13:5, 52:8).*

- I am saved by His mercy and not by any work of righteousness. *(Titus 3:5).*

- I am delighted that as it is written, goodness and mercy shall follow me all the days of my life. *(Psalm 23:6).*

- I am trusting the LORD that He may have mercy

upon me: for the LORD is a God of judgement, blessed are all that wait for Him. *(Isaiah 30:18).*

- I am delighted that those who trust God will be encompassed with mercy. *(Psalm 32:10).*

- I am assured that all the paths of the LORD are mercy and truth to such as keep His commandments. *(Psalm 25:10).*

- I am grateful that God pardons iniquity and passes by the transgression of the remnant of His heritage because He delights in mercy. *(Micah 7:18).*

Confessions on the Mind

- I am thinking of things that are just, things that are pure, things that are lovely, things that are of good report, and things that are of virtue. *(Philippians 4:8).*

- I am one with the Divine Mind of God that holds a solution to every problem. *(Philippians 2:5, 4:13).*

- I am requesting daily that the LORD renews a right spirit within me. *(Psalm 51:10).*

- I am requesting daily that the Holy Spirit imputes purity into my understanding, thoughts, imaginations, desire, intellect, heart, soul, mind, brain and actions. *(Psalm 51:10; Psalm 119:32)*

- I am confident that the LORD will keep me in perfect peace as I keep my mind focused on Him. *(Isaiah 26:3).*

- I am blessed with the peace of God which passes all understanding keeping my heart and mind through

Christ Jesus. *(Philippians 4:7)*.

Confessions on Peace

- I am blessed with the peace of God which passes all understanding keeping my heart and mind through Christ Jesus. *(Philippians 4:7)*.

- I am daily exalting my Lord and Savior Jesus Christ, our Prince of Peace who broke down the wall of partition between us and our Father and so made peace by his blood. *(Ephesians 2:13-15)*.

- I am serving the Author of Peace who daily blesses us with His grace and peace. *(Colossians 1:2; I Thessalonians 1: 1-2)*.

- I am exhorted as a believer to pray for Kings and all that are in authority so that we may lead a quiet and peaceable life in all godliness and honesty. *(I Timothy 2:1-2)*.

- I am anchored by the Prince of Peace who gives me serenity during trials and brings stability to my life. *(Isaiah 9:6)*.

- I am grateful for the peace of God that brings resolution and restoration to my life. *(Isaiah 57: 19)*.

- I am praying for the peace of God to rule my heart always. *(Colossians 3:15; Philippians 4:7)*.

- I am being prepared for my eternal destination and the certainty of my heavenly home fills my heart with peace. *(Hebrew 6:19)*.

Confessions on the Tongue

- I am warned that the tongue can set on fire the cause of nature and it is a world of iniquity that defiles the whole body. *(James 3:6).*

- I am admonished that "he that will love life and see good days, let him refrain his tongue from evil and his lips that they speak no guile". *(I Peter 3:10).*

- I am striving not to sow strife among my friends or gossip to stir up dissension and separate close friends. *(Proverbs 16:25).*

- I am enabled to keep my tongue from evil and my lips from speaking lies. *(Psalm 34:13).*

- I am purposed to avoid endangering my neighbor's life with gossip. *(I John 2:10-11).*

- I am striving not to betray anyone's confidence with gossip. *(Leviticus 19:16; Proverbs 20:19).*

- I am hidden from the scourge of the tongue. *(Job 5:21).*

- I am preserved from men who have the poison of asps under their lips. *(Romans 3:13).*

- I am delivered from evil men who have sharpened their tongue like a serpent's tongue. *(Psalm 140:3).*

- I am determined to keep my tongue from evil and my lips from speaking guile. *(Psalm 43:13).*

- I am praying for the tongue of the wise which is health. *(Proverbs 12:18).*

- I am praying for the gift of a wholesome tongue

which is a tree of life. *(Proverbs 15:4)*.

Confessions on Wisdom

- I am in agreement with the Bible that the wisdom of this world is folly with God. *(1 Corinthians 3:19)*.

- I am certain that the fear of God is the beginning of wisdom. *(Psalm 111:10)*.

- I am daily confessing wisdom as my defense because wisdom gives life to them who have it and it is the stability and strength of my salvation. *(Ecclesiastics 7:12; Isaiah 33:6)*.

- I am daily reaping riches and honor as fruits of wisdom. *(Proverbs 8:18)*.

- I am assisted by the Holy Spirit to allow His light to shine in my heart to give me knowledge and wisdom. *(II Corinthians 4:6)*.

- I am assured that the LORD gives wisdom, knowledge and joy liberally to all who ask. *(James 1:5;Ecclesiastics 2:26)*

- I am taught wisdom in my inward hidden place by the power of the Christ in me. *(Psalm 51:6)*.

- I am praising the LORD who counsels and instructs me with wisdom even at night. *(Psalm 16:7)*.

- I am daily coveting wisdom because it is better than rubies, and all the things that may be desired are not to be compared to wisdom. *(Job 28:15; Proverbs 3:14, 7:4, 8:11, 16:16)*.

- I am seeking the wisdom that is from above which

is pure, peaceable, full of good fruits without partiality and without hypocrisy. (*James 3:17*)

PART IV

CONFESSIONS ON CHRISTIAN VIRTUES

Chapter 14

Confessions on Christian Virtues

...Not by might, nor by power, but by my spirit, saith the Lord of hosts.

Zechariah 4:6

Confessions on Forgiveness

- I am allowing the forgiving love of God to express itself freely through me, cleansing my mind with its mighty power. *(Luke 6:37; Matthew 6:14).*

- I am allowing each act of forgiveness to set me free as I release others *(and myself) from resentment in my heart. (Colossians 3:13).*

- I am comforted that God said: "If my people, which are called by my name, shall humble themselves and pray, and seek my face, and turn from their wicked ways; then will I hear from heaven and will forgive their sins, and will heal their land. *(II Chronicles 7:14).*

- I am serving the God who forgave all my iniquities and healed me of all diseases. *(Psalm 103:3).*

- I am encouraged to forgive because of the word which says, "Father forgive them; they do not know what they are doing." *(Luke 23:34).*

- I am mindful of the command: "Bear with one another forgive each other ... the Lord has forgiven you, now you do the same." *(Colossians 3:13 NJB).*

- I am delighted with the assurance of God's forgiveness that says, Although we were dead because we were sinners, He has brought us to life with Christ and He has forgiven us every one of our sins. *(Colossians 2:13).*

- I am proclaiming the good news that "If we confess our sins, He is faithful and just to forgive us our sins, and to cleanse us from all unrighteousness". *(I John 1:9 KJV).*

- I am affirming the ultimate truth that "we have redemption through His *(Jesus) blood, the forgiveness of sins, according to the riches of His grace"* . *(Ephesians 1:7; Colossians 1:14).*

Confessions on Faith

- I am a child of God through faith in Christ Jesus. *(Galatians 3:26).*

- I am living by faith and not by sight. *(II Corinthians 5:7).*

- I am fixing my eyes on Jesus Christ who is the author and finisher of my faith. *(Hebrews 12:2).*

- I am admonished to make my requests with unwavering faith because those who ask waveringly do not receive anything from God. *(James 1: 5-6)*.

- I am enabled to ask with deep faith, without any doubt, knowing that he who doubts is like a wave of the sea that is blown and tossed by the wind. *(James 1:5-6)*.

- I am enabled to be on my guard and to stand firm in faith and be strong through Christ. *(I Corinthians 16:13)*.

- I am daily letting go of all burden and I am trusting in the transforming power of faith. *(Hebrews 6:12; 11:20)*.

- I am believing the words of our Savior that if we have faith as small as a mustard seed we can move mountains. *(Matthew 17:20)*.

- I am enabled by the Holy Spirit to walk by faith and not by sight. *(II Corinthians 5:7)*.

- I am enabled to forget things that are past and to press forward by faith to the high calling of God in Christ. *(Philippians 3:13-14)*.

Confessions on Patience and Perseverance

- I am affirming that as it is written, "You have need of endurance so that when you have done the will of God you may receive what is promised". *(Hebrews 10:36)*.

- I am waiting on the LORD with patience just as the

farmers wait for the later rain because He is faithful that promised. *(Hebrew 10:35).*

- I am propelled by my joyful hope in Christ. *(Isaiah 43:18; Philippians 3:13-14).*

- I am imitating those who, through faith and patience, inherited what had been promised to them. *(Hebrews 6:12).*

- I am holding patiently to the hope I profess knowing that He who promised is faithful. *(Hebrews 10:23).*

Chapter 15

The Call to the Kingdom and the Sacred Commitment

*D*ear Father, the Great I AM THAT I AM, Creator of all things, I bow before you in humility and adoration. I am aware that you are a holy and merciful God and that out of mercy you sent your Son with the WORD to redeem man from the clutches of Satan and deception. I am aware that Jesus suffered and was nailed to the cross for bringing salvation to mankind.

I accept the sacrifice of his innocent blood that he shed for me on the cross in atonement for my sins. I believe that you raised Jesus from the dead and He is now sitting on your right hand as our High Priest. I believe that I will be raised to life because of his victory over death. I know that the death and resurrection of Jesus paved the only way to enter your Holy Presence. Through Jesus, I have been plucked out of darkness to become a member of the Family of Light and Love. Hallelujah!

I willingly submit my life and choose to make Jesus Christ, the Savior and the Lord of my life, the center of my existence and the controller of my destiny. I ask for the Holy Spirit to enter and fill me and change my life from this moment.

I promise to love God the Father with my whole heart henceforth and to serve and obey Him as commanded.

Thank you for the precious gift of salvation and eternal life. All glory to you, the only Uncreated, Living and Self-sustaining God, in Jesus name. Amen.

THE SACRED COMMITMENT

I _____on this day (*date*)_____ earnestly and joyfully make this sacred commitment, with the help of the Holy Spirit in me, to give thanks, praise, and worship to the great I AM, my Father, Creator, and Healer, for at least 15 minutes each day of my life. Amen.

DOXOLOGY

> "Now unto Him who is able to do immeasurably more than all we ask or imagine, according to the power that is at work within us, to Him be glory in the Church and in Christ Jesus throughout all generations, forever and ever. Amen."
>
> *Ephesians 3:20-21.*

www.ingramcontent.com/pod-product-compliance
Lightning Source LLC
Chambersburg PA
CBHW031558040426
42452CB00006B/348